LEVEL UP YOUR TEENS

DARREN HORNE

WWW.DARRENHORNE.COM

FIRST EDITION

Darren Horne
Snapchat @darrenhorne
Twitter @darrenhorne
Instagram @darrenhorne77
Linkedin @darrenhorne
Askwhale @darrenhorne
Website www.darrenhorne.com

Book Layout ©2017 BookDesignTemplates.com
Cover Design: Just Call Me Doc and Raya Rose Design

Level Up Your Teens/ Darren Horne. —1st Ed.
ISBN 978-1542610797

Contents

Dedicated to:
My supportive wife Emily, my feisty daughter Evelyn,
and anyone who feels as though they are struggling to
deal with life

.

"When sorrows come, they come not single spies.
But in battalions."

Shakespeare

PREFACE

Evelyn was born. She was born on 13th January 2016, and everything changed for me.

At first it was not in a good way. I was diagnosed with Post-Natal Depression (which I did not even know men could get) and spent the best part of a year fighting back.

I took time off from work, went on medication (yes, anti-depressants), changed my diet for a while (ketogenic), read many books, and went on courses. I levelled up, because being a father was too high a level quest for me. I just wasn't prepared.

And I should have been. My wife and I had been together for nearly ten years, we were, and still are, married (not that it's vital to be), and the pregnancy was planned. We both have good jobs, a great support network, and Evie was healthy. I had nothing to complain about as I had won the lottery of life.

But I still got depression. I felt trapped in a bubble and the love and laughter happening around me just could not get in. We nearly divorced several times, but we got through it.

This was the darkest time in my life, when it should have been the brightest.
I was the product of an education system, and society, that had completely let me down.

Why wasn't I taught the skills at school to just deal with life?

All of the important things seem to be off the curriculum, and most of the skills we need are about how to deal with our emotions.

Such as how to manage those feelings of love, heartbreak, and unrequited love. How to talk to someone who is bereaved. How to deal with miscarriage, anxiety, depression, loneliness.

What about how to deal with parenthood and the overwhelming emotions that can bring on? I am in a place now where the feeling of love I have towards Evie is painful. I ache with love. Some kind of training in how to surf that emotion would help, just in case I get the urge to pull a *John Wick*, in a scenario in which it really isn't required.

Sadly it seems that modern education is no different, and that anxiety, depression, body dysmorphia, and suicidal thoughts, and attempts, are all on the rise.

The statistics are terrifying.

1 in 10 children have a diagnosable mental health disorder – that's roughly 3 children in every classroom (i)

1 in 5 young adults have a diagnosable mental health disorder (ii)

Half of all mental health problems manifest by the age of 14, with 75% by age 24

Almost 1 in 4 children and young people show some evidence of mental ill health (including anxiety and depression) (iii)

Suicide is the most common cause of death for boys aged between 5-19 years, and the second most common for girls of this age (iv)

1 in 12 young people self-harm at some point in their lives, though there is evidence that this could be a lot higher. Girls are more likely to self-harm than boys. (v)

Young Minds

The Government know what is wrong with the education system, but they don't care. In January 2017 Prime Minister Theresa May announced mental health reforms to focus on young people. But the focus was on providing support, not on finding out the cause!

Imagine if all the children were bleeding, and the Government just provided more plasters? How about we look at the cause? What is it about the education system, society, diet, and media influence, that is making our children sick?

By the age of three or four some children have already pretty much begun to make up their minds (and even hold strong views) about how bodies should look. There is also research evidence to suggest that some 4-year-olds are aware of strategies as to how to lose weight.

Dr Jacqueline Harding

Surely the Government do not want to create an obedient population that is trained to sit at a desk eight hours a day, be afraid of failure, have little creative thinking, no understanding of how politics or the banking systems work, slaves to their emotions, and just intelligent enough to work 40+ hours a week until they die?

No. That would be crazy.

But, this book is not a rant on the education system. It's a way for me to share some of the skills I have learnt to deal with life. I want you to get the most out of your time on the planet, to not let fear control your destiny, and to develop the skills so that you can fulfil your dreams.

Even writing a book. You can do that too.

What follows are a series of life hacks and signposts that I hope will help you get the most out of life, get in the game, level up, be all you can be, or whatever metaphor you want to go with.

My students, and teenage followers on Snapchat, seem to think I can be of use. Sure I am nearly 40, and have a child and wife and a kinda grown up job. But that just means I am now in the mentor stage of my life and I want to share what I have learned.

And why should you listen to me? Well, I have been teaching media for over a decade, and I understand the impact it has on its audience. My students have been very kind to me, and often encouraged me to write a book, do motivational talks, or start life coaching.

I have a fair bit of life experience and have had many different jobs in the past. Even now, I teach, run a martial arts studio focusing on life performance, I do life coaching, and I am about to be an author. But really I have been in a battle with life for decades. My recent post-natal depression made me realise I have had social anxiety and bouts of depression for my whole life. I nearly lost that fight. Nearly lost my family and nearly went broke. But I survived by piecing together some of the strategies you will read about in this book.

Since the end of 2016 I have realised I have the tools to be happy, and I can live the life I want to. If I can do it, you can do it.

I am a level 40 warrior, and I care. I have been on this journey and I have wise advice that can help make your path easier.

Life can be amazing. But it needs a lot of us to work together to make the world the place it has the potential to be.

I hope you like the book. I have kept it short, and easy to read. You can read it from front to back if you want, or just dive into whichever chapter takes your interest.

Please feel free to reach out and connect with me on social media. It would be great to hear from you.

Email: darrenhorne@live.co.uk
Website: www.darrenhorne.com
Facebook: www.facebook.com/darrenhorne77
Snapchat: @darrenhorne
Twitter @darrenhorne
Instagram: @darrenhorne77
Youtube: @darrenhorne77
Linkedin: www.linkedin.com/in/darrenhorne

CHAPTER 1

Why This Book Is The Book You Are Looking For

"The children now love luxury. They have bad manners, contempt for authority; they show disrespect for elders and love chatter in place of exercise."

Socrates

Every older generation eyes teenagers with distrust, and will lament to anyone that will listen that young people do not realise how good they have it.

It appears that nothing changes, but is it really all that great to be an adolescent in the modern world?

I have been teaching in the post-compulsory education sector for 10 years and have witnessed, first hand, the changing challenges that you are facing. The most concerning of which are growing mental health issues. In fact, my job has become less about teaching a curriculum and more about trying to keep my students alive.

Education lets you down

We offer a Victorian-era education system which teaches obedience and conformity; with over-testing used routinely, too much homework to allow time to explore outside, or indulge in hobbies, and a lack of real world valuable education.

I once asked my students how much they thought I got paid. *"Oh you must be on at least £8 an hour!"* No wonder they don't value education when they think after a master's degree and teacher training I would only be on a few pounds more than them.

You have been let down by your schools, and also your parents. We have a duty to talk about our wages, debts, interest rates, bills, and savings.

Learning should be life-long, but our passion, our confidence, self-esteem, curiosity, and motivation, are all too often stamped on in secondary school.

> Too many children have become vulnerable, scared of life, as they learn more of the dangers 'out there' instead of being excited by its opportunities and challenges.
>
> Peter Tait (Headmaster)

Of course the media plays its part, as we are assaulted by its negativity from birth. So why is there no media education (or, as I call it, Defence Against the Dark Arts) in primary school? It should be mandatory in secondary school, and taught by media specialists, not an English, Performing Arts, or in one instance I heard of, P.E teacher, "making do".

Information overload, too much choice leads to boredom

Teenagers today can do anything. You can watch any movie, listen to any music, investigate any subject, and communicate with people all over the globe. So sadly, many of you do nothing.

It's too big. Hick's Law states that the more options we have the longer it takes to make a decision. And with the lack of belief in yourselves, no wonder some of you decide not to choose at all.

It stuns me how often I see teens on Snapchat snap "someone talk" or "bored". Many are alone and scared, but will never admit it. But how can you make a decision when you also don't know what to believe? More and more people are waking up to the fact that maybe, just maybe, the media has an agenda.

Emotionally unsupported

Emotionally intelligent people are more likely to succeed but it's not something that is supported in our teens, in fact, quite the opposite.

> Emotional intelligence is the cornerstone of mental strength. You cannot be mentally strong without the ability to fully understand and tolerate strong negative emotions and do something productive with them. Moments that test your mental strength are ultimately testing your emotional intelligence (EQ).
>
> Travis Bradberry

Our teens overvalue other people's opinions and allow negative people far too much influence on their state of mind. You have been taught that failure is a terrible thing, and are scared to try new things in case you make a mistake. Because of advertising and social media you over-compare with other people, usually negatively.

You don't exercise as much as school playing fields are sold off, and contact sports require too much health and safety insurance. You, in no way, get enough sleep. In fact there is evidence that teens should not start school until 10am.

Misunderstood by adults

I am often asked why teens are disillusioned, and I am always surprised at the question. Just take a moment. You are told you will probably be living with your parents until you are 30+, you are told jobs are hard to get, university is expensive (and besides there are graduates working in retail alongside you on minimum wage), the things you love doing are not valued, and the media has been brainwashing you to be unhappy with your bodies and possessions since you were born.

Life is very different now. You can make money online, you can be a digital nomad, you can play video games for a living (why is it weird that there is a market in watching people play video games? Don't people watch snooker, golf, chess?) You can be an entrepreneur at fourteen now.

R.I.P patience; you want the perfect life now

Even I hate waiting. When Netflix buffers for just a few seconds I get impatient. What must it be like for a generation that has grown up with the ability to watch anything immediately, or have next day delivery, or instant gratification from playing videos games?

Remember the Stanford marshmallow experiment where children were offered one marshmallow (or other treat) now, or two in fifteen minutes? The children that could delay their gratification turned out more successful in life. That was in the 1960s and 70s. Our teens are programmed for instant gratification in the modern world.

Pornography

Even mainstream media is now basically soft porn in parts. Advertisements, music videos, magazine covers. Sex is everywhere. Throw in very easily accessible and problematic hard core pornography and you have a generation of young men that see women as objects to be dominated, and young women that feel pressure to be a circus performer in the bedroom. Thankfully groups like www.FightTheNewDrug.org are working to educate people about the dangers. Porn kills love after all.

Sure we can say that you've never had it so good, and a lot of this is first world problems, and some teens are making it through unharmed. But too many of you are in pain, and need support and empathy.

The above may feel negative, but on the plus side you have bought, borrowed, or are sneakily reading in a shop, this book.

I don't have all the answers, and I won't even address every one of those problems. But I will offer some tips on how to combat them, and point you in the direction of some amazing resources.

Because actually, with a little help, it can be amazing to be a teen in the modern world, and you really can smash life.

CHAPTER 2

You Are The Hero Of This Quest, Not An NPC

"A journey of a thousand miles begins with a single step"

Lao-tzu

6 • DARREN HORNE

W hat if I told you that the hundreds of hours you have spent adventuring in the games like Skyrim was actually time well spent learning to hack life?

As a media specialist, I see it as part of my job to stay up to date with the gaming industry, or at least that's what I tell my wife.

I think it was *Ultima IV* on the *Sega Master System* that first got me hooked, and with each generation of consoles the worlds became richer and richer. From *Shining Force* on the *Megadrive*, *Final Fantasy* on the *Playstation One*, to the awesome depth and characterisation of the next gen consoles, in my case the Xbox One, and games such as *Skyrim*, *Witcher,* and *Fallout.*

If I added up the hours I have spent exploring dungeons, finding treasures, and defeating evil, I might wonder why I didn't spend that time learning a new language or instrument, or seeing more of the real world. Thankfully that time was not wasted for I have learned valuable lessons.

You have to keep gaining experience points

Everything you do in Role Playing Games (RPG) is about getting experience points (XP), as this is the key to becoming the hero you will need to be to complete the adventure. At the beginning these XP have an immediate impact.

Even killing a small animal such as a mudcrab might be enough to level up. The problem in life is that we often stop seeking out new adventures in order to get this much needed XP.

I managed a wonderful independent cinema in Penrith, Cumbria, for eight years and I sadly see that some of that time as treading water. I already had management experience in pubs and a theatre, and had excellent customer service skills. So once I learned the culture, back office, and technology of the cinema, I really stopped learning.

In *Skyrim* I never settled down in one place and did the same thing over and over again, and if I did I would expect the challenge to increase as I grew more skilled. Sadly the cinema never increased its difficulty level (other than moving from 35mm to digital) and so I coasted.

The cinema was a low level quest barely worth my time after that first year (as much as I loved the job). But if you take on too big a quest, the reward might be great in terms of XP, but you will probably die. Self-awareness is key, what level quest can you handle but is also enough of a challenge to get something from it?

Keep improving your stats

We need XP in order to invest in our stats and attributes. Through experience we can increase a wide range of skills such as stealth, archery, or lock picking. Sure, those are not exactly vital in everyday life, but why don't we focus as much energy on developing our actual abilities?

Sadly we do not have an easily available character sheet to see how we are doing, or even better, a heads up display that we can bring up to see a detailed breakdown of our skills, even if it's in cooking, nappy changing, driving, article writing, or any other activity we spend time doing.

When we play games we want to max out as many skills as possible, but in life we hate doing things we are bad at, we are impatient in terms of wanting immediate results, and we don't get a cool notification when we have made progress. This is why it is important to build relationships with people who can support you and comment on your achievements.

Look out for opportunities to level up

In *Skyrim,* when you get enough experience points you level up. And it's glorious. Early in the game it happens pretty regularly as everything is a challenge. When you were a baby everything was an adventure. You went from immobile, to rolling, crawling, and then walking in probably less than a year. What have you achieved this year that can match that?

But a baby is just starting out and is level 1, whereas you are much higher and need to find dragons to kill to test your ability. We need to keep pushing our comfort zone and challenging ourselves.

Even when we finish a game, many of us play it over again at a harder difficulty level. But in life we can coast, settle, tread water, and then wonder why our lives are not exciting any more. Fear is often associated with levelling up, so jump at those scary opportunities.

Explore your environment

In life we follow the same paths every day. We really don't explore that much. We go from our homes, to work, to the shop, and to a friend or family member's house. And yet in *Skyrim* I will spend a ton of time climbing a mountain just to see what's up there.

In games we are curious about the world around us and we do not feel like we have got value unless we have explored every part of it, we even try and get to places we think the game doesn't want us to go. Take some time just to walk or drive around where you live, you might find a beauty spot, or a charming cafe, or maybe even the love of your life. If you have the chance to visit a city or country that you have not been to, go! Just to see what's there.

Go on side quests and have variety

In *Skyrim* you have the main mission. To save the land from the evil dragon *Alduin*, and you could probably finish the game fairly quickly if you just focused on that. But where is the fun in that? No, you need to go on a ton of minor missions and side quests. Who knows what treasures you will find?

What is great about *Skyrim* is you can also fulfil major quests that are completely unrelated to each other. You can join the Thieves Guild and then become its leader, likewise with being an assassin for the Dark Brotherhood. However you might also join the Companions as a mercenary for hire, or join the Imperial or Stormcloak Armies to help them ensure victory in their war. You can even go and become the Arch-Mage of the College of Winterhold.

You get to play out several diverse roles and yet in life we can often be pigeon holed. We think that the job we have is for life, or that's all we can do. But it's not true. You can do anything any other human being has done, and quite possibly something no one has ever done. So fulfil your main quest, but look out for side missions.

There is no reason you can't start a business, or write, or have an online store. My "proper job" is a media lecturer, but I also run a martial arts studio, I have a life coaching company, and have now also decided to be a writer.

If I can run the Dark Brotherhood Assassins Guild, and be Arch-Mage in *Skyrim*, I don't see why I can't do diverse things in life. And neither should you.

Talk to as many Non Player Characters (NPCs) as possible

There are two elements to this. One is a life hack I use quite often, and that is thinking of the possibility that all of you are NPCs in the game of my life. You have set things you can say and do, and you are just obeying your programming. I should therefore not get frustrated when you say the wrong thing, or block a doorway and not let me through (okay that one would bug me).

The other part of this is how much effort we spend meeting NPCs. In any given town in *Skyrim* I will not leave until I have spoken to everyone, just in case they have important information, maybe a new mission, or just even say something amusing. And yet in real life I can be at a party and will speak to the same three or four people, or be waiting in a supermarket queue and won't talk to the person next to me. So many missed opportunities to connect with people, which could change your life for the better.

When you get hurt, seek a health potion

Okay this one might be a little more focused on me. In 2016 when I got post-natal depression, I remember having a breakthrough in fighting it when I started to think of the points I have made in this article. I related it to being poisoned or cursed in *Skyrim* and accepted I would not be operating at my usual 100%, and I had to do whatever I could to deal with it. But I didn't mind as I was on a quest and I told myself I could fix it, just as I would in *Skyrim*.

And that's what I did. I spoke to new people (doctor, counsellor), sought out health potions (antidepressants and a better diet), went on appropriate quests (became a Neuro Linguistic Programming Practitioner), found and read magical texts (Matt Haig's *Reasons To Stay Alive*) and I got it under control. So don't accept a negative state, whether its fear, anxiety, depression, or illness. Get experience points, raise your stats, level up, explore your environment, go on side quests, and talk to NPCs. Get back to your 100% health.

So that's it. Don't let all those hours of game play count for nothing. You can use that experience to rock your real life and remember you are the hero of your own game. Level up your character.

CHAPTER 3

Answer The Call To Adventure

"A ship in harbor is safe, but that is not what ships are built for."

John A. Shedd

Now that we've established that you're the hero of your life, what does that mean? Surely you need some kind of quest? Conveniently the structure of your journey has been laid out for you already, so all you have to do is follow it...

The hero's journey

Joseph Campbell wrote *The Hero With A Thousand Faces* in 1949, in which he studied vast amounts of stories across the planet, and realised that they all had the same structure. Civilisations that had never met had the same characters and the same plot points.

But that book is heavy reading. I have two degrees, and I did not get through it. Let me know if you do though!

Thankfully Chris Vogler, who was working for Disney at the time, came up with a more accessible version, which became *The Writer's Journey*. He applied the theory directly to films, particularly *Star Wars (1977)*, which might have been what caught my attention.

The theory is quite simple, but can be applied and used in different ways.

"At heart, despite its infinite variety, the hero's story is always a journey. A hero leaves her comfortable, ordinary surroundings to venture into a challenging, unfamiliar world.

It may be an outward journey to an actual place: a labyrinth, forest or cave, a strange city or country, a new locale that becomes the arena for her conflict with antagonistic, challenging forces"

This is a great structure to help in script writing, but it is also genuinely a guide to dealing with life. His book is over 400 pages, so this is a very brief introduction to it.

But go check out the book yourself. It's a great read.

Below are some key stages of the Hero's Journey that can be applied to your life.

The ordinary world

This is your current state. You are happy here, safe, and well provided. Why would you leave? It's Luke on Tattooine, Frodo in the Shire, Katniss in District 12, and Moana on Motunui.

Sure you may be a little dissatisfied, but it's the world you know, and talk of leaving is all too often, just talk.

So your ordinary world is your current state, whether that's single or in a relationship, skilled or unskilled, in work or out of work.

It could be your home town, or even your school, as much as you may hate it. When my students leave the security of their school, and choose to come to the college to continue their study, I think of them as rock stars! They left a building they knew, the teachers they knew, and went into the unknown. That takes a tremendous amount of courage, but too often they think of it as nothing. Likewise with going to university outside of your home county. Do you even realise it's your hero's quest?

Now, how many adults do you know that hate their ordinary world but won't leave?

They spend eight plus hours a day dragging themselves through a soul-destroying job they despise, get home mentally and physically exhausted, can't be bothered to cook so get a takeaway or have microwavable meals. One glass of wine turns into a bottle.

They grit their teeth and push on, just hoping to get to the weekend where they can get black-out drunk, and recover just in time for Monday when they can start their own personal hell once more. Repeat for decades until death (let's face it; retirement becomes less and less likely every year).

So much sadness and unfilled dreams. But unlike the banker father in *Mary Poppins*, no one is coming to save them.

There is a great scene in *Jack Reacher* in which the title character looks across to a grey office block at the workers sat in office cubicles, with fluorescent lighting, staring at computer screens, and asks if they are really free.

Call to adventure

In life we get many calls to adventure, some obvious, some rather subtle. It's unlikely to be an owl with a message, or an R2 unit with a message from Princess Leia.

It could be a job advertisement, a smile from someone you are attracted to, a flyer for a marathon, a university prospectus, a positive pregnancy test, maybe your car breaks down, or you go overdrawn and get a warning email. It doesn't matter. For me it could even be my daughter crying in the night.

Refuse the call

I could be tempted to refuse that call, and my mind will come up with all kinds of excuses. "She will go back to sleep," or "it's not my turn," but my mentor or ally (wife) gifts me with a kick, and I answer the call and cross the threshold of the bedroom which is safe and warm.

I go in to the dark, cold hallway, and I approach the innermost cave (nursery), and I am tested trying to find the artefact (dummy) in the dark where Evie has thrown it.

I have an ordeal getting her back to sleep, and return to the bedroom triumphant for a rewarding cuddle and gratitude.

How much more fun is it to think of it in those terms? And how we think about things, will affect how we feel about them too.

We all get the call and it is okay to want to refuse it. It's often linked to a negative emotion such as fear, laziness, and lack of compassion. If it's not scary or challenging, it's probably a too low a quest. It's often fear of the unknown.

But even the low level quests have some value, such as washing up or cleaning. Doing that well and mindfully develops self-control and discipline. Two things you will need on bigger adventures.

This is also where we might 'mind read' unsuccessfully. We convince ourselves there is no point because we assume the answer is no. This happens often in relationship quests.

In movies this refusal might be subtle. Maybe the hero's hands rests on a doorknob and she takes a breath before turning it.

Or maybe it's like *Lord of the Rings* when Samwise Gamgee pauses and says that when he takes one more step, he will be the farthest he has been from home that he has ever been.

How exhilarating is that?

So you have the call, but do you answer? The beacons have been lit, are you Rohan? Will you answer the call?

Now, in most narratives the hero needs a push. So she will seek out a mentor (or the mentor randomly pops up). The mentor is usually older and wiser, such as Gandalf, Merlin, Yoda, Dumbledore, Obi-One Kenobi, or more fittingly for me, Hamish.

In real life your mentor might be… Well me, obviously. But also an older sibling, parent, friend, teacher or someone online such as Gary Vaynerchuck, Erica Blair, or Eric Thomas.

The beautiful thing about the modern world is you can actually connect and build relationships with these people, not just consume content. One of my mentors is Kevin Kruse, and he is the reason this book exists.

They can give you support and advice. But often they will also give you a gift. In films it could be a wand, a lightsabre, a shield, sword, magic cloak, training, or even just advice. In our lives it could be money, a lift, a book, an item of clothing such as a tie or dress, a Snapchat account to follow, it doesn't matter. The important thing is that if you look closely there are mentors all around you, showering you with gifts. The challenge is identifying the right ones.

Incidentally, I was having a low point during the writing of this book, as I was getting bogged down in the legality of permissions and how and when you can quote other people's work, as well as formatting and cover design. I lit the beacons last thing at night, and shortly afterwards my mentors and allies came to my aid.

Kevin responded and explained how he formatted his books, my Snapchat friend Josh Kotoff (@mrscifiguy) offered to do cover design and a day later sent me a mock up that was awesome, and Chris Vogler responded. A guy who was my mentor, but never knew it, reached out and said I could use selected passages in this book and also said that the Hero's Journey was a great template for commercial scripts, but it's really there for life coaching!

BOOOOM! What a guy! The world is full of kind, helpful people. You just need to filter them in.

So now you are the hero, you have been called to action, and you have your mentor and your gift. It's time to go on the quest and cross the threshold.

Crossing the threshold

Yes! This is when the story gets going. We are on the adventure! It has started! We are in the Falcon flying off to see the Universe. Or on the bus on the way to university.

It's deciding to ask that boy out, to enter the competition, fill in the application form, learning to drive, to have a baby.

This is now new territory, and this is the start of LEVELLING UP!

Well done!

So what's stopping you from succeeding?

Tests, allies and enemies

On your journey you will, of course be tested, and you will meet allies and enemies. The allies will help you on your journey, and include characters such as Han Solo, Bucky, and Hermione.

Tests might include external enemies such as rival suitors, mercenaries, and weird, tribal, coconut creatures. Which in our world could be unhelpful call centres (being on hold is the hero's torture scene), traffic jams, an unhappy co-worker, or a recipe you are using to cook for a date. Or enemies within, such as doubt, anxiety, fear, hate. That's where the real battle happens, right?

But there are many stories that take the hero on an inward journey, one of the mind, the heart, the spirit. In any good story the hero grows and changes, making a journey from one way of being to the next: from despair to hope, weakness to strength, folly to wisdom, love to hate and back again. It's these emotional journeys that hook an audience and make a story worth watching.

Chris Vogler

Approach the innermost cave

Eventually you will approach the place of the major challenge. This is the Death Star, the Temple of Doom, or The Hunger Games.

For us it could be the interview, the date, the competition. On the approach we ready our minds and make sure we have everything we need. Quite often there is a moment to relax. To strategise and refuel.

To maybe consider the consequences of the next step. You might be tempted to bail at this point. Sitting in a room waiting for the interview or to see the dentist. Maybe you are off stage waiting to give your presentation, perform a song or theatre piece. It's common to throw up at a time like this.

But you feel it, right? You are on the verge of something great!

The ordeal

This is where it gets bad. This is the big test and the hero often comes very close to death. Moana and Maui get smashed by the lava monster, James Bond has his genitals tortured, and many romantic endeavours come close to crashing and burning due to some kind of misunderstanding.

Life loves giving out a kicking, but if we can take it and don't give up, greatness can happen on the other side.

Reward, road back, resurrection, and the return with the elixir

You did it! You overcame the ordeal, killed the dragon, saved the day, and can now claim your prize. In films it could be a special artefact, the love interest, lifting the curse etc.

But it could also be wisdom, insight, or understanding.

In life maybe you got on the course, passed the test, got the girl, made the film etc. But now you have to get home.

Often the hero is now pursued home by enemy forces. She may even have another life and death experience. Even when the end is in sight, you do not want to drop the ball. If only they realised that in *The Mist.*

You get to bring the reward back to your community and family. How will you use is it? Do your parents accept your new partner? Does your new job fit in with your other responsibilities? Perhaps you can even mentor other potential heroes now?

The key thing here is you get experience points, you LEVEL UP, and you come back changed. The journey should change you. In a very obvious way Tristan in *Stardust* changes his exterior, in terms of clothes and hair style, as well as his abilities as he can now sword fight, but he has also changed his interior because he is now confident, and has knowledge of the world.

But it has to be a challenge. Otherwise, why would you refuse it to start with?

So that's your heroic journey, but remember you are also sometimes the mentor to others, and sadly sometimes the villain. Be aware of what role you are playing at any given time and make sure that it is your decision to do so.

I use this all the time. My wife knows it too. I was having a tough week fairly recently and I had so much to accomplish. And she said, "but you are approaching the cave aren't you? This is your end of level boss?"

Sure, she mixed metaphors a bit there, but it still worked. I stood taller, imagined a broadsword on my back and prepared for battle. And I accomplished my quest.

It's fun to see real life challenges and people as villains, tricksters, mentors, and allies. You probably do it already don't you? You refer to people as trolls, dragons, witches, princesses, your squad, and more?

It can be enough to get you off the sofa and on the road to glory!

CHAPTER 4

Casting The Spell Of Imprisonment

"Worthless people live only to eat and drink;
people of worth eat and drink only to live"

Socrates

I am fascinated by choices. And options.

I suspect there is something in human nature that means we do not like choices, as a great level of freedom is actually kind of terrifying. Since having a daughter I am often pushed for time, so it's wonderful when I get a two hour slot and take the opportunity to watch a film.

So what do I usually end up watching? Yep, an episode of a TV show, because it takes so long to decide which film I should watch that I run out of time.

When I was in my teens, I had a couple of VHS videos and four channels on the TV. My choices were limited, but I always found something to watch. Fast forward to now, and I have over a hundred channels, I have Netflix, Amazon Prime, YouTube, and more.

Too much choice, too much freedom, can paralyse us. So we limit our options in order to function and not be overwhelmed.

However, you shouldn't limit your choices too much as this can cause you to feel trapped in life.

Let's look at three ways we choose to use language that enslaves us.

There is a third option

We impose limited choices on ourselves all the time. Students will think they have two options after college, go to university or get a job.

Really?

REALLY?

Do not make that decision until you have written at least ten options down. This **could** ('could' is a great word, much better than 'should') include charity, or travelling, or starting your own business, or trying to make money via You Tube or Twitch.

When you are young you have time. I wouldn't suggest it, but you can mess up the next six years of your life and probably do no real damage. Your responsibilities are minor right now, but once you have a family and bills it all gets a bit trickier.

But even with that list, your brain is going in to lock down trying to shut down the possibility of you achieving those options. "I **can't** go travelling without money"? Can't you?

How much money do you need? Research, and do a budget. Can you travel around China teaching English as you go? Pick fruit in Australia? Where do your family and friends live? Can you sofa surf around America or Europe? Can you sell old toys and clothes to raise the flight fare to get you started?

The problem is that we like limited choices. Remember, Hicks Law states that the more options we have, the longer it takes to make a decision.

Often parents, teachers, people in sales, and authority figures will try and make you think you have two options. Even my wife does this. She will say "Baby, (she calls me baby sometimes) do you want to put the rubbish out or do the washing up?"

And I see what she is doing and so I choose a third option. "I want to sit here and watch the Warrior again."

She didn't see that coming! Boom! (I put the rubbish out.)

With my daughter, if she doesn't like broccoli, I won't say, "do you want some broccoli?" I will say, "Do you want two pieces of broccoli or three?"

I spoke to my father just recently and a salesman tried limiting his options on the phone. "We have a sales rep in your area on Tuesday at 3pm or Friday at 9am, which one is most convenient for you?"

You have to have your guard up; the world is full of snakes. Thankfully my dad caught the trick and chose a third option, and got rid of the salesman. As in, hung up on him, not… you know… killed him.

Start filtering in when it feels like the "system" or your own mind, is trying to limit your options, and make sure you are okay with that.

There are two great examples I have come across in moving image. One is the movie *Snow Piercer*. (There is a great breakdown of this film by *Every Frame A Painting* and one by *Nerdwriter1* on You Tube.)

Snow Piercer is a superb film that uses a train as a metaphor and microcosm of the world. Chris Evans and his friends start at the back of the train and live in total poverty. They decide to make a break for it and fight their way to the front of the train where they think things will be better. And in many ways they are correct. They fight past school classrooms (spewing out propaganda), sushi bars, tailors, dentists, a rave, and more. The further they go the more decadent things get.

The whole film has Chris Evans looking back (left of screen) from where he has come from, and forward (right of screen) to where he wants to go. His choice is always; do we give up and go back, or keep going forward despite heavy losses?

Once he gets to the front he realises that they are all trapped in their place, and all have a role to play. And he can now be at the front, but in order for that to work someone has to be at the back.

We see this in many films. Another favourite is *In Time*, where for a few to live forever, many must die (in our society, for a few to be incredibly rich, many have to be poor). People know their life span, and earn time by working, and spend their seconds, minutes, and hours on coffee, rent, and clothes.

Which is really what we all do, isn't it? How many minutes would you need to work to earn enough money to buy a coffee? What about new trainers?

What's interesting in *Snow Piercer* is that there is a character played by Kang-ho Song that does not just look backwards and forwards. He understands there is a life outside of the train, a third option.

So often we get so wrapped up in playing the rules of the game, we forget it's just a game and we can flip the table if we choose.

How can you apply this to your life? Don't let other people's words or beliefs imprison you.

Question everything, even to the absurd level.

Why do you eat cereal for breakfast? Because you grew up doing so? Cultures all over the world eat different things. Why can we have bacon or sausages for breakfast, but not a steak?

Check out the film *Life in a Day* to see how other people are living their lives, but also how humanity can be beautiful, and we have more in common than we think.

We're all prisoners in one way or another

Seems dramatic, right? But there is truth in this.

I have seen this lot with the students and clients I coach. They imprison themselves by saying, "I can't do presentations," and so it becomes a self-fulfilling prophecy. Your brain goes, "yep, okay, message received. We can't do presentations".

"Can't" is a dangerous word to be throwing around. So is "never" and "always", as well as short phrases such as "have to".

Watch out for those words and phrases and re-program yourself to feel happier.

The consequences are often not as bad as you think. *Feel* what happens when you change the words of the spell. If you say, "I **should** have done the washing up", it may be tinged with regret, guilt, or sadness. Then change it to, "you **could** have done the washing up", how is that different?

Words are magic that cast spells every day, on yourself and others. If you can learn to use them correctly you can really hack life.

But now you are probably reeling off all of the consequences that might happen because of your decisions. They really, are often not that bad.

I will use myself as an example.

I **have** to go to work. If I don't I will get fired, and I won't be able to pay rent, and then I end up homeless, and can't eat and die.

Do I?

If I don't go to work for one day. Nothing happens. I just have to fill in an absent form saying I was sick. If I did it regularly I might get a disciplinary and a warning. But to paraphrase Brad Pitt in *Inglorious Bastards*, it's not like I haven't been disciplined before.

Eventually, I might be fired.

And then I would have lots of time to look for a new job that I **choose** to go to because I enjoy it.

If that didn't happen we might need to move in with parents for a while, as I look for work, or start a business, or whatever I **choose** to do.

Sure, these are not great options, but many people have fulfilled their dreams **after** being fired or dropping out of college.

The point is, when I say I **choose** to go to work, I feel better about it. And if I do not want to do that job; well I need to do a side quest in my own time to eventually replace it. If I don't want to work 40 hours a week full stop, then I better start looking at multiple income streams and passive income. I have tons of options. I just need to communicate with myself in words that filter those options in.

Whenever you are faced with something you feel trapped by, and want to escape, try asking yourself what the consequence would be. Say to yourself "and what happens then?" Then say it again, and again, as you answer each question.

The final outcome is usually not that scary, and will help you to stop worrying as much. Choose to choose.

Not my circus, not my monkeys

I follow Stoicism. Kind of. I guess I mean I have read a few books and 'liked' the occasional meme. I have watched *Gladiator* quite a few times (Marcus Aurelius' is in it, played by Richard Harris).

And one of the key beliefs that I take from Stoicism, in particular a dude called Epictetus, is that some things are within your control and some things are not. So why are you getting worried or anxious about the things you cannot control?

In the past I have had bad managers who would send an email last thing on a Friday night saying "we need a meeting" on Monday. So I would spend the whole weekend worrying about what it was a about. What a waste of time that was!

We can do the same waiting for exam results. It's no longer within our control, so don't worry.

The global political arena right now (May 2017) seems to be fuelling an awful lot of talk of nuclear wars, world wars, and more.

There are people getting into heated social media arguments, over things they have no control over. Why?

Some things are within your control and some things are not.

One of the main things within your control is how you respond to the events of life. But I appreciate that takes practice.

Epictetus said that "it's not events, but our opinions about them which cause us suffering." Captain Jack Sparrow said something similar.

We also mix these beliefs with mind reading or fortune telling. "I can't ask for that because they will say no," or, "she would never go out with me".

Again we are choosing and limiting our options. Why concern yourself with things that do not concern you? Or things that you actually have no control over? Or choosing to assume how someone is going to react?

I see a lot of this happening around me, and it can be the cause of a great deal of suffering.

.

CHAPTER 5

Armour Up!

"Anger. Control your anger. If you hold anger toward
others, they have control over you. Your opponent can
dominate and defeat you if you allow him to get you
irritated"

Miyamoto Musashi

I am sure we have all heard that the clothes maketh the man, but do we really pay enough attention to it?

There are plenty of stories in which people respond to someone in a uniform, a high visibility jacket, or a doctor's lab coat, with subservience or agreement, just because of what they were wearing.

So don't be so impressed by someone else's armour that you can be swayed into doing things that you do not agree with, and stop applying your critical thinking skills.

And think about your own armour and the impact you want it to have in life.

External armour

You have two types of armour, internal and external. Your external armour is perhaps the most obvious and the easiest to engage with. So for example, let's say you are not feeling great about the day's challenges, or an interview you have, or a date. Armour the hell up!

It's a quest! You are the hero. Dress appropriately.

In the case of an interview you should, if you can, buy new and appropriate clothes. Wearing new clothes is like getting into a bed with fresh sheets on. It feels amazing and makes you feel happy and confident. You need to bring your best self and new clothes will help you do that, make you feel successful and of value.

If you cannot afford that option, then at the very least wear freshly laundered clothes. Maybe go as far as ironing them? This is your

Batsuit. I love a good armouring-up scene. My fave might have to be Arnie in *Commando*.

Likewise with how you get to the interview. A bus? No. What is your Batmobile? Imagine how successful you would feel being chauffeur driven, or driving a Ferrari. Sure, we can't go that far, but there is a happy medium.

All these things have an impact.

You should also shower, and shave. I would even trim your finger nails and make sure they are clean. Does this really help? Yes! Well, according to the movies.

I still remember watching Season Two of *24* and seeing Jack Bauer shaving and cutting his hair, as a sign to all that he was back and ready for action.

To feel strong I dress for the apocalypse and I always want to feel battle ready. This has become even more important since having a daughter as my timetable is not my own. This is also because I have watched *Die Hard* too many times, and being caught barefoot in a "terrorist" situation and having to run over glass, is not my idea of fun.

So my ideal clothes are boots, jeans, and a t shirt. I wish I could teach wearing that, because I feel much more comfortable. But no, we have a staff dress code, just as pupils in school have a uniform.

They say that a uniform prevents bullying, but was that your experience? Or should you be able to express yourself creatively through what you wear? And if you are to blame for being bullied for that choice, well, isn't that victim shaming?

School uniform is all about teaching obedience and stifling individuality.

But for an interview I would suit up, but it depends. You will need to research the culture. There are stories of new media companies that want to break so much from tradition that a suit would make them not want to hire you.

Anchors

We use anchors all the time in terms of what we wear. Or how we "design" ourselves. What do you wear to anchor yourself to a feeling, belief, or sense of identity?

Here are some of mine:

1: My boots are actually my younger brother's boots. He is a Royal Marine Commando and one of the most self-sufficient, confident, and capable people I know. They have the name Horne written in them, along with a number. When I have those boots on they become an anchor to the positive traits I see in my brother.

Literally, Adam could handle this, and so I can too. I like the way they sound when I walk, excellent footstep noise.

2: Wedding ring. Sure, a lot of people have wedding rings, but how much thought did they put in to them? Mine is made of titanium, and it looks like a tarnished silver metal with XVI XII

MMX111 inscribed along the outside. They are the roman numerals for the day I got married. The ring is an anchor to faith, strength, loyalty, and love. I run it with my thumb absentmindedly and it gives me strength, as it's also an anchor to the man Emily sees in me.

I also love stories about warriors, such as knights and samurais. So it probably won't come as a surprise that I got married in a castle. Yep, a 15th Century medieval Scottish castle. I have a sword with our names engraved on them. Because I am a Knight, and Emily is my Queen, and I shall stay loyal to her.

3: Tattoos. Everyone seems to be getting tattoos these days. I have two. The first, a raven, I got whilst at art college (Plymouth College of Art and Design) in my teens. I was heavily into, um, magic, at the time. Yep, I was reading up on Wicca, delving into mythology, rocking the Ouija board, and more.

The raven was inspired by Odin, who had two, Huginn and Muninn. They would fly around the world and bring Odin news and knowledge. I am also sure I read that if you swore something in the name of Odin, and broke that Oath, the ravens would come and peck your eyes out. It stayed with me.

My second tattoo is an engraved-in-stone effect of the logo of a modern martial arts brand called Crazy Monkey Defence. I had been studying it for a few years, and had become a trainer, and decided to get the tattoo because of the physical and emotional impact my experience had on me.

But the monkey tattoo has several meanings to me. A symbol of evolution, playfulness, and being part of a tribe or troop. But also a warrior, a reminder that I can manage my emotions in stressful situations such as sparring, and I know how to use those skills I learn on the mat (mind and body management) off the mat.

This anchor keeps growing and gaining new meaning. Conveniently my daughter was also born in the Chinese year of the monkey, and the book the *Chimp Paradox* has had a profound impact on me too.

Anchors can also tie in to a goal. If you really want to visit New York, get a keyring of the Empire State Building as a constant reminder that you have a goal.

If you want to give up smoking, change your password on your computer to "I don't need to smoke", so every time you log in you are telling your mind that statement. Your screensavers and desktops should be anchors to your beliefs and goals as well.

What are you wearing right now? Do you feel strong?

Internal armour

You have armoured up. You have the right clothing for the task at hand, you have a couple of anchors to remind you of who you are and what you believe.

Now what?
Well, you need to get that volcano of emotions and thoughts under control. So let's rock some internal management skills.

Mind-body connect

Breathe. It's a bad day, not a bad life.

So what is this "mind-body connect"? Put simply, how you hold your body can have a direct impact on how you feel. Have you ever felt ill in bed, and thought you could not possibly deal with the day, but then you forced yourself up, and after a few minutes felt much better?

Amy Cuddy is a Harvard Business School professor and social psychologist.

Amy did a TED.com talk which is the 2nd most viewed TED talk of all time, where she shows that if you hold a Wonder Woman pose for two minutes, your testosterone levels go up, and your cortisol levels go down (my wife has a Wonder Woman keyring as one of her anchors).

Which means you feel more confident and less anxious.

Try it.

In self-defense sparring we call this "body attitude". If my body flinches, cowers, looks weak, my mind will follow. If I project strength, stand balanced and strong, my mind will be calm and confident. This also has an impact on my opponent.

If I do not react to being punched, did I get punched? The opponent will not be sure.

At night, when your mind is taking you on laps of insecurity, anxiety, stress and worry, do not stay in bed. Do not just lie there and let your mind have a civil war. Get up. Call on your body as reinforcement.

Just standing tall will have an impact. I shadow box. Even for twenty seconds it has an impact. Try doing press-ups. Remind your mind and body that they are strong, and they will rise to the challenge.

Mindfulness

Mindfulness is on the rise. There is a lot of talk about it and it can get misinterpreted. To put it simply, mindfulness is paying attention to what is going on in the present moment.

I am a trainer in a martial arts system called Crazy Monkey Defense. Its founder, Rodney King, has integrated what he calls "mindfulness in action" throughout the system. I don't have to be sitting on a bean bag meditating to be mindful, I can do it while sparring.

> "Mindfulness is never about avoiding experiences you are having now; but rather, it is a way to help you become aware of your in-the-moment experiences, exactly as they occur.
>
> For many people, the insight that is gained is liberating, to know that you are not your thoughts and feelings, and that you can choose how to respond, rather than having your thoughts and feelings respond for you on autopilot."
>
> Rodney King

Life is amazing. It really is.

But we can be dragged along by our own thoughts and emotions, and end up places we do not wish to be.

If you can observe your thoughts and your emotions, they cannot be you. They are just passing through.

We also have a reticular activating system (look it up!) which filters in the world. And we need to program what it focuses on. So, for example, after we got married, my wife suddenly wanted a baby.

I really did not see that coming.

But for me, kids were annoying. The only time I noticed babies was when they were screaming.

But when I started to be more aware of my surroundings, I could filter in the positive examples, and I started to realise there are many wonderful, kind, polite, well-behaved kids all around. It's the same when you buy a car. I bought an Audi TT and suddenly I see them everywhere. EVERYWHERE!

So what are you filtering in and out?

Are you focusing on the bad news? The violent stories, the fear mongering? That means you can start to think the world is much meaner than it is.

The whole way you view the world can change, just by changing what you focus on.

The film *About Time* is a fantastic example of this. The main character can go through the day rushed and stressed, consumed by his own chores, or chose to take a moment and admire the architecture of the building they are in, smile and chat to the person selling coffee, and realise how thankful he should be.

There are many films that can capture that moment of serenity (I think even *Serenity* does?) where the heroes know a terrible thing is about to happen, and they stop panicking, relax, and experience the moment non-judgementally.

The most powerful scene in *Toy Story 3* is moments before they think they are meeting their death, Woody, Buzz, and the rest of their companions, reach out and hold each other's hands. They accept the situation without negative emotion.

But the master of all examples of film mindfulness is George Clooney in *Gravity.* He is floating out into space, and is going to meet certain death. And a rather nasty death too. But he looks around and is heard on the radio to say what an amazing view he has.

Absolutely badass! I think one of the main missions in life is to prepare for our death. How are we going to handle it? I love all those alleged final words of movie stars such as Humphrey Bogart, "I never should have switched from Scotch to Martinis," and Errol Flynn, "I've had a hell of a lot of fun and I've enjoyed every minute of it".

I hope I am that cool.

But mindfulness is not just about facing death. Although it's a great time to deploy it, so you can think logically rather than emotionally. It's also about doing the task at hand well.

Samurai films often show this well, whether it's older films directed by Akira Kurosawa (director of *Seven Samurai*), or more recent ones such as *The Last Samurai*.

Taking a moment to focus on the present often means you enter a flow state, where time flies past and your mind is calm. This is common in sports, but you can also have it in computer games (which explains how it suddenly hits 3am). Imagine if you could do this at any time?

I did it recently at the dentist. Over two hours in the chair for a root canal, but I basically stepped back from my thoughts and emotions and watched with curiosity what was happening in the present.

Every time my thoughts went to the future or the past I brought them back to the present. I allowed emotions to come and go, with inquisitiveness. Not attaching any value to them. When I heard the drill start up, my mind would jump to the future and start reacting to imminent pain. But I picked up on it, used the mind-body connect and relaxed my tensing body, breathed, and brought my thoughts back to the present, where there was no pain.

Even when there was pain, it was over fast. So what should I do, keep thinking about the last time it hurt? Nope.

This allows us to take a break too. If you are making a cup of tea, make the cup of tea!

Take a moment. Don't check social media. Boil the kettle; allow it to cool for a minute or two. Pour the water in to the cup. Wait. Breathe. You are making a cup of tea right now. Work can wait. Stress can wait. Deadlines can wait. They will all be there waiting.

Slowly take out the tea bag, add in the milk as required, and watch as it merges and settles.

Take a break. Make, and drink, a cup of tea.

It is so much better than racing to make it, checking you phone in one hand, boiling water sploshing out of the kettle into, and around, the cup and your body getting tense, as your mind gets stressed.

You don't have to pretend to be a movie samurai like I do, but give mindfulness a try.

CHAPTER 6

Time Travel, And Not In A Good Way

"If you really want to escape the things that harass you, what
you're needing is not to be in a different place,
but to be a different person"

Seneca

Time is an odd little thing. Sometimes it moves fast, sometimes slow, we have so little of it, and yet waste most of it, or sell it too cheaply.

Time for money

My students get jobs that pay around £6 or £7 an hour. But then they have to factor in travel costs, travel time, buying perhaps multiple coffees, or having to pay for lunch whilst at work. They are then often so exhausted from working in a job that they are not passionate about, that some then comfort buy treats, such as clothes or tech, or self-medicate with alcohol or cannabis.

So really, what are they actually earning for that time? You have earned money, if you have saved it. If you have put in somewhere that it is actually making you money, for example earning interest. That's YOUR money. Anything else is just living expenses.

So, how much is your time worth?

Imagine a parent or family member is ill, and does not have long left to live. How much would you need to get paid to not be at their bedside?

What about if you have children? How much will you need to get paid to not spend time with them, to see them grow up?

Hell, what if you buy a puppy! How much would you want to get paid to not spend all day playing with it?

£6-£7 an hour just does not cut it. You need to start thinking now about how much your time will be worth when you are older, and how you are going to make yourself that valuable.

Do not let your age hold you back. Plenty of teenagers start companies, become millionaires, give TED talks. You can too!

Future love

One of the biggest issues I see with people, not just teens, is a lack of love for their future selves.

Imagine if you could travel through time, and go twenty years into the future, see your future self and give them a hug. Say "I love you", and here is £20,000 I saved for you. Or here is a passive income I have built up through multiple income streams so you don't even have to work if you don't want to.

Now imagine if past you did that. If eight year old you could travel through time to the present and say that they had decided to save half of their pocket money, Christmas money, chore money etc. and they had saved £2,000 because they loved you.

Would that help you now?

So why not do that for future you?

We know the reason. Current you is kind of a dick.

Current me can be too. And in the past that was certainly true. Which of these applies to you?

- "I will leave this essay until the last minute, this essay is future me's problem"

- "Yes I will stay up late into the early morning playing this game. Being tired for work tomorrow is morning me's issue"

- "Wow, I have logged 150 hours playing this game. I could have learned another language, instrument, coding in that time"

I know I have been guilty of all of those at some point in my life. But having a daughter has changed all of that. I now think twenty years in to the future with ease.

Will she have to do a minimum wage job she hates? That's not why I brought her into the world, and I hope that's not the reason your parents brought you into the world.

We do this with far scarier things than essays, games, and money. We do it with health. We are self-harmers, all of us.

We all knowingly consume food and drink that we know is bad for us and will cause issues for our future selves. Crappy processed food, sugar filled energy drinks, alcohol, cigarettes? We lay on sofas binge-watching escapist TV, avoid exercise, and sit at desks for eight hours a day doing damage to our bodies that one day we will have to account for.

But that's future you's issue. So why care?

How much patience do you have? One of the most hope-filled movies that regularly gets into the top ten lists is *Shawshank Redemption*.

Andy goes through hell in prison, but spends time each evening tunnelling through a wall. He does this for nearly seventeen years. Each night, very slowly working towards his goal.

What can you do today that will achieve a goal in twenty years? Even if its ten minutes a day? Can you spare ten minutes?

Future you can also be a dick. You can have great intentions and put into action wonderful plans. You can order that book from Amazon, but future you needs to read it. You can decide to change your way of eating, but future you needs to stick to it.

You need to check mate your future self. Work out how to hack your mind.

Tyler Durden pulls off the ultimate check mate in *Fight Club*. He commands his men to castrate him if he tries to change the plans in the future. Seems a little intense to me.

So, you probably can't afford to hire someone, and having someone cut your balls off is definitely a level of commitment I would not suggest.

But you can get accountability partners. Tell your friends and family what you intend to do. Since January I have been telling anyone who will listen that I will publish a book by summer. So they ask me about it, send me articles and tips on how to achieve it, and encourage me.

You can send out ripples. Light the beacons! Arrange to meet allies and mentors for coffee. I am sure I read or saw in an interview that Ben Affleck and Matt Damon would have business meetings every week, before they had made it. They had nothing to discuss, but they knew it was important to have that mind-set.

What is stopping you from winning? Your Xbox? Give it away today. That will show future you!

One of my hacks is to help others. I encourage those around me to write a book and give them advice, and somehow that rebounds on me. I help people fight depression and anxiety, and you know what happens? I get better at fighting it!

So pause from reading this book, light the beacon in any way you see fit, and put future you in a position where she will feel obligated to help you on your quest.

Past hate

We give away too much power to the past, and in the wrong way. We hang on to all the negatives, and allow it to cause unhappiness in the present. This, I have realised, is crazy.

Let's look at memories, oh those evil memories.

Memories are insanely unreliable. It's basically that game you might have played at school where someone whispers a statement into your ear, and you whisper it into another person's ear. And so on for twenty people. Is the statement you started with the same as the one at the end?

Each time you access a memory you change it. You exaggerate it or diminish it to suit your agenda.

So you had a hard time at school. Each time you think about it, it becomes a little bit more extreme. Bit by bit. Like Andy digging through the tunnel.

The language we use reinforces it. "My teacher hated me". Hated? Hate? That is really strong language to use and colours the memory.

A useful tool I learnt with problematic memories is to re-edit them. So bring up the memory and let it play through. Let's watch an episode of My Bullying Hell At School.

So close your eyes, in a minute, after reading this paragraph. And watch a bad memory. Where is it? Is it all around in virtual reality? Is it loud? Full of colour? Sensorama?

DUDE! It's your memory! Let's shut that down if its doing you harm.

So let's give it a frame. Make the screen smaller. Move it away from you and put it in a little TV. Now it's contained at least.

Is the bully loud? What's that in your hand? A remote control? How handy.

Let's mute that douchebag. That's better right? Is the memory still intense? Okay let's drain some colour from it; maybe turn it black and white? What happens if you speed it up and go fast forward? What happens if you turn the sound on but raise the pitch so the bully sounds like Alvin and the Chipmunks?

It's your mind. Your memory. If it causes pain, re-edit it!

Present understanding

Language is magic. It's crazy that how we communicate and describe our world defines its meaning

How old are you?

In a month I will be 40 years old. Why do we use years? How does our relationship with time change if we describe it differently?
I am 40 years old, or nearly fifteen thousand days old. How I write it changes it too. What's longer, fifteen thousand days or 15,000 days? How old is an eighteen year old? Not even seven thousand days.

Maths is fun, right?

If you are 18, when did you "come online"? When do you think you were starting to be you? Weirdly most people I ask do say it's in their teens (I usually say a year ago). So, you might have only been "online" for three years. Maybe less. So just over a thousand days old? And you are expected to know what you should do with your life?

Give yourself a break. You are young. Fresh out of the academy. You are not supposed to know it all. And you are just in the tutorial walk through of this game. Don't judge *Fallout 3* by life in the Vault!

Kevin Kruse often writes about how many minutes are in the day. 1440. That's what we all have. What are you going to do with yours?

So you might have slept for 480 of them. So you have less than a thousand. And they are ticking down.

Highly successful people break down their time in terms of 15 minute slots, for maximum productivity.

Take away the meals, travel time, toilet breaks, bathroom routine etc. How much is left?

This is your life…. ticking away.

Why would you ever waste it?

I do this with my daughter. The average amount of time that Evie sleeps for during the day is an hour and a half. How long is that? When I think of it in those terms, she sleeps, I kill some time, play on an app, go on social media. Chill out. It's quite a long time right?

But it's actually only 90 minutes. Now its 89 and I haven't even washed up from breakfast yet. Now its 82 and I still need to shower. There is urgency when you see a countdown counting down. That's why movies use them so much… Time is ticking.

The film *In Time* does this beautifully. If you had a countdown on your arm, counting down your life in decades, years, days, hours, minutes, and seconds… What would you do today?

Time goes slower when we think about it. If I am sparring and willing the timer to go, that's a loooooonnnnnng round. If I am in the moment, it flies back. Mindfulness can be time travel.

We also overthink. Trust yourself.

I love movies, and once timed how long it took Keanu Reeves character in *Point Break* to jump out of an aeroplane without a parachute... Less than 10 seconds.

Sure, I know it's a movie. An awesome movie. But a movie. But how often have you had to make a decision, had a gut feeling, and then procrastinated for days, weeks, months, and came to the same conclusion as you had after 10 seconds?

How much time do you even have? You might have time now, but think you have time tomorrow, so put off tasks today and relax.

But life changes! It develops and things happen!

You cannot be sure how much time you have tomorrow, so when given the opportunity to do something, start today!

We put things off and screw over future selves.

If the deadline for an essay or application was three months from now. when would you start it? A couple of days before the deadline, right?

WHY?????????

Just do it now. You don't know what the future holds. What if you get ill or you get in to a relationship and disappear from the world in a loved up Buffy and Riley lust haze?

A cool lesson of productive people is that if something takes less than ten minutes, do it now! I have been doing that for a few months and it's amazing how useful it is. Its helps keep your slate clean of minor irritations that you can easily forget about, and yet will cause stress in the back of your mind.

CHAPTER 7

Who Is In Your Apocalypse Squad?

"The key is to keep company only with people who uplift you, whose presence calls forth your best."

Epictetus

A key part of any adventure is putting together your team, your squad, your fellowship, tribe, troop, or gang. Who you surround yourself with is a key part of who you will be. It may not be your actual apocalypse squad (although I do have one of those) but it is your team to help smash the challenges of life.

Your apocalypse squad is the team you want around you when the, well, apocalypse hits. I usually get drawn to the zombie versions, ideally *Shaun of the Dead* or *Zombieland*, rather than *28 Days Later* or *World War Z*. But *Mad Max*, *The Mist*, or even the future world in *Terminator* can all work. Put it simply, when all hell breaks loose, who do you hope you will be in the room with?

So now imagine you are about to enter this life. This world. And you are putting your squad together. Who would be in it?

Audit your friends

Take an audit of your five closest friends. Are they good for you?

Be honest.

Imagine if your five friends were Mark Zuckerberg, Bill Gates, Elon Musk, Justin Kahn, and Warren Buffet. You would be rich, right?

Apply this to any field. Acting, music, construction, law, politics. In fact politics is a great example. How many "politicians" earn great money for doing very little, because they went to school with the Prime Minister?

Now let's look back at your friends.

This is harsh isn't it? But if you are unhappy with your life and you want change this is important. If you want happiness, success, and confidence then you need to make sure no one in your inner circle is a frickin Sith Lord. Someone spewing out negativity, and doubt, and holding you back.

Sadly... That might even be your parents.

If you drink too much alcohol, and all your friends do, are you really going to cut back?

If you are trying to get fit, but your friends aren't, how easy will that struggle be?

I cannot stress the importance of this enough. We see it all the time as lecturers. A really bright student, full of potential, starts hanging out with the students who are not that motivated or talented. Their potential dies.

Or, the other way around, a student who scraped onto the course, has no real talent or knowledge, but randomly sat next to one of the brightest students we have ever had. Suddenly they are rocking it.

That's how I did great at university. I was a mature student, and so naturally made friends with the other mature students. In particular a guy called Jason. We were each other's pace car, setting the commitment, standard, and level of effort.

We supported and competed with each other. We both got 1st class honours degrees. If Jason was not on that course, I can't be sure that would have happened.

I understand that removing negative influences will be a challenge if they are your best friends or your parents. So it would be best to have a conversation. Tell them what your goals are, and highlight how their lack of faith, criticism, or perhaps even fear, is impacting you. If they love you, they will listen.

Maybe they worry your dream is not possible. So? You are young. You have time to try and fail. Or compromise and have a safety net or side hustle. If you are trying a new trapeze act, you have a net in place until you get the hang of it. So maybe reassure your parents with a net of some kind?

Are you Superman and Wonder Woman?

This is also true of your partner. Are you and your boyfriend/girlfriend a power couple? Do you support each other, and does your whole equal more than the sum of your parts?

You need to be like the Power Rangers or any group that can merge together to create a super being! 1+1 = a bazillion!

Superman and Wonder Woman are often described as a power couple. Are you in a power couple?

If not, can you help your partner level the hell up? Are they holding you back because your success makes them feel bad, or unworthy of you?

This is common. If one person goes off to university, meets fascinating people from diverse backgrounds, experiences new things, and levels up, whilst their partner stays in their home town, doing the same things they always did. Is that going to work?

It can. Of course it can. But start filtering in that scenario when you see it. It sure is a challenge.

My wife and I met when I became the manager of a cinema. She was a part-time front of house worker, and immediately caught my attention. That summer we flirted, and by the end of the year we were a couple.

Since then she has levelled up greatly. She went to university and got her degree, then her masters. She got an internship at the NHS and was promoted several times before switching over to the police and tackling new challenges.

She is a bright and brilliant communications specialist, and has given birth, so any martial arts macho posturing I do really does not impress her much. She tried a Brazillian Jiu Jitsu class at my studio once. Another client said they were worried about hurting her, she replied, "I have given birth, nothing you can do to me compares to that".

That's my wife.

Absolutely badass!

So, would we be together if I was still at the cinema? Maybe.

But it helps that I levelled up. That I own and run a martial arts studio, have started life coaching, and now I'm a writer.

We support each other, but we are also each other's pace cars.

Is your partner a pace car? Are they supportive, always growing, and encouraging you to do so too?

Some people are very threatened when their partners level up past them. Don't let that be you.

Mentors and allies

Who are your mentors? Might I suggest a few?

Of course, this will depend on what field you aim to smash! But I do think there are some mentors who can cross boundaries and help you no matter what field you are in.

What we all need most, is a cheerleader.

We could all probably do with some help with social media too, and modern technology. The world is changing and changing fast.

So here are my four top tips of people you can follow, learn from, or engage with on social media.

Kevin Kruse

Yep. Kevin. A guy I now weirdly count as a friend, even though I had never heard of him before December 2016. Kevin is a New

York Times best-selling author and Inc 500 Entrepreneur. He is all about the power of intimate attention, basically connecting with people and helping them when you can.

This book exists because of Kevin. Any success I have in 2017 and into the future will probably be down to him. Sure, I executed, I actually did the work. But he showed the way.

So why should you follow him?

He is a genuinely nice guy!

I think the people you come across that can be your mentors will generally have the same mission as you. Kevin wants to, as his book jacket says:

> Provide life-changing hope and help so others can achieve their potential
>
> Kevin Kruse

His latest book *Text Me, Snap Me, Ask Me Anything* has his phone number, Snapcode, and email on the front cover. And he responds!

Kevin wrote an article for Forbes, about the top 17 Snapchatters you should follow. I followed them all. He encourages his followers to write a book, and to start by writing articles. But he did this on Snapchat, which somehow makes it feel as though he is talking to you. He said teachers should definitely write a book, as they already have a subject matter specialism. That really got my attention.

So I wrote a few articles and put them on *Medium.com*. Kevin liked them and asked me to write for *LEADx.org* which is:

> [...] a digital mixed media company that provides professional knowledge and training for millennials and others who want to achieve their full potential.
>
> LeadX.org

This is pretty much my mission statement too.

He wants you to win. Go check out www.LeadX.org for tons of great articles and podcasts for FREE.

Website: www.KevinKruse.com
Snapcode: @kevinauthor

Gary Vaynerchuk

Gary is the reason I am on Snapchat. I am not even sure how I came across Gary, but when I did, his high energy, sweary, in your face motivation certainly connected with me. He is also the reason I played with *Musically* for a while.

He is the CEO of *VaynerMedia* which is a highly influential and sought after digital agency, among other things.

He pushes the envelope of what's going to be the next big thing, and is open about his losses too. He has MASSIVE audience engagement and a film crew that follows him around filming the *Daily Vee*, as well as that he now has a call in show where, if you are lucky enough to get chosen, you get to ask him a couple of questions.

If you watch enough of his videos you will no doubt spot his influence throughout this book. He wants you to be self-aware, authentic, patient, and hustle. He also listens to young people to see where the attention is.

Google his *Mondays* video for a taster to see if he works for you. But also go back and check out his first *Wine Library* video. We are all bad when we first start. You make good films by making bad ones, write good books by writing bad ones *cough, cough*.

Do not judge yourself against Level 40 arch mages. That's dumb. Compare yourself to them when they were the same level as you, if at all.

Website: www.GaryVaynerchuk.com
Snapchat: @garyvee

Alan Watts

Alan is an author, speaker, and was one of the first to interpret Eastern wisdom for Western audiences. I came across him via one of those motivational montages put together with one of his talks. The key one being, *what would you like to do, if money were no object?*

For me, what you do in your free time is what you should be doing all the time. At the weekend, on Bank Holidays, during summer holidays between academic years.

My students returned from Easter break and I asked what they did, because that could impact what they will do. Only one or two made a film, a few others took photographs, and others wrote. They are the filmmakers, the photographers, and the writers. The others, probably, are not.

So what did the others do?

I don't mind. If they played computer games the whole time, well, find a way to earn a living from it. People do, but you will probably need to be serious about it. Gain a following, create a brand, study tactics, advise others, enter competitions etc. It can be done.

Sure you might fail, but I think it was Jim Carey who said that you can fail at doing something you don't want, so you might as well try for something you love.

That was my biggest take away from Alan, and I go back to his videos regularly. I have a few of his books too, but at the moment his level of philosophy can be a little over my head.
But, if I am ever sitting in a garden, care free, watching a sunset, it will be his book I reach for.

Website: www.AlanWatts.com

Simon Sinek

Simon is an optimist, who believes we can build an amazing future together. All of us. He is a good influence to have in your life.

You might have already come across him on social media due to his "millennials" video, where he talks about the challenges that those becoming adults after the year 2000 are facing. His talks are engaging, funny, and insightful, and are well worth watching.

He also talks about the "why?" Why do you do what you do? He applies it to companies, which, he thinks, are more successful if they have a strong belief, or "why", rather than greed.

He suggests you probably know your "why" around the age of 16. This is the age where you are pretty much formed, and are starting to engage in the world. The media, society, parents then create white noise that leads us away from what our calling is.

I only recently had that breakthrough. So try not to make the mistake that I did. When I was a teenager I loved films and role playing games and dungeons and dragons. I thought it was film that was my passion, and when I went travelling around South East Asia I sought out cinemas wherever I went so I could keep consuming film.

I thought I wanted to work in film, and make film. So I went to university, got my degree, then a master's degree as well. Thankfully when I asked a mentor what they thought I should do after graduating they said I should teach. I said "really?" and she replied something like, "Darren, you are a teacher; you have been doing it all year."

And I guess I had, but I just had a passion for film, and was a little older, and so was happy to help other students.

So I went into teaching film, with a heavy dose of production. I loved the teaching, but not the film making. What was that about?

Recently I found a blog I wrote in 2011 on the importance of levelling up. And it all started to click. I didn't love films in my youth; I loved the hero's journey, and good people overcoming evil. That's what I wanted to do, not act in a film or make a film, but live my life as though I was living the film.

To hear the call to adventure, find mentors, seek allies, and level up my skill tree. Now, typing this I am 39. I am teaching the media I enjoy as a lecturer.

I am writing articles for LeadX.org who want to help you get 1% better each day.

I run a martial arts studio helping my clients build physical and emotional resilience through stress inoculation and mind management techniques, and I am writing this book.

My "why", is helping you achieve your full potential and be the hero of your journey. To not be afraid of the unknown, and to stand up against the unfairness and cruelty we sometimes see in our society. Simon Sinek helped me realise that.

Website: www.StartWithWhy.com

CHAPTER 8

Why It's Awesome To Be Adventuring Now

"The object of life is not to be on the side of the majority, but to escape finding oneself in the ranks of the insane."

Marcus Aurelius

It is awesome. It really is. Sure I can tell old man stories of four TV channels, hiking out to *Blockbuster* to rent videos that might not be in stock, or be mysteriously "deleted", no internet, hanging out by phone boxes, and that sex education was *Kays* catalogue, *Eurotrash*, or a soggy porn magazine found in a wood.

I have suffered!

But you? You have the world! So what's AWESOME about now?

Total accessibility to your mentors and heroes

Through social media you can legitimately reach out and make connections with virtually anyone. Especially if you are young because you can leverage that to get some attention.

You can be mentored by billionaires if you want!

Sure, you could read books about Edison, Tesla, and Marcus Aurelius, but it's not the same as personalised video. Snapchat changed the game. Justin Kan is the creator of Twitch, which he sold for so much money, it's crazy to count. Whilst on his exercise bike he would get bored and answer questions on Snapchat.

He would answer questions!!!

But a lot of those questions were the same, so he set up a new app called Ask Whale where tons of influencers, tech geniuses, founders and... me, can get asked a text question, and answer it via a video of up to 60 seconds. And it's mainly free right now!

Do you understand how crazy that is? Just get the Ask Whale app, search whatever area you are interested in and find a mentor to advise you. You totally can win!

Even without apps like Snapchat and Ask Whale, you can find your heroes on Twitter, Facebook, Instagram, and more.

Just reach out. Ask them for advice.

Ideally do something for them first. Even if that's following them, commenting, or sharing. Do that for six months and then make a request.

Let them get sense of who you are and have an online profile so they can see you are "good people".

Sure nine out of ten might say no. But one might say yes. My students have been doing this a ton. Hooking up interviews with YouTube influencers, make up gurus, and more.

Digital nomads

You can now work from anywhere in the world, with an internet connection and a laptop. There are so many ways to make money online, and what's crazy is that you can get so much more for your money in other countries. Sure, £500 a month is not much in the UK, but how about Chiang Mai in Thailand?

You can run websites, blogs, translate, do photography and put them on sites like iStockPhoto for sale, write, create art, do graphic design, affiliate marketing, an online shop, teach, coach or tutor, be a virtual assistant, and so much more!

Check out Fiverr, Upwork, and People Per Hour for job offers.

Hell, not to get too maudlin, but if you get left a house in a will, rent it out, and go live in South East Asia for a few years.

You can be location independent and have a wonderful time in beautiful locations. You can do that, YOU! Is this your call to adventure? What is stopping you? What fear?

Way more support for LGBT+

This is a wonderful change that I have witnessed, and not just in the big cities. Sure we can focus on the darkness and the hate and prejudice, but I see way more people being comfortable with who they are, and more accepting of those that are different than them.

The internet allows you to find like-minded people and communities for support. More and more characters are appearing on television in which their LGBTQ status is not a fetish or a punchline. Check out *Kiss Kiss Bang Bang*, *Orange Is The New Black*, *Modern Family*, even some NPCs in *Witcher 3*.

Streaming

You can watch anything! I thought Netflix was a scam when I first got it. I could not believe I got access to so much content for £5.99 (which it was back then).

Sure I see people say "oh but there is nothing to watch". Fools!

What you mean is there is nothing you KNOW for sure you will like to watch. So try something new. I have found so many gems. *Always Sunny In Philadelphia, Jen Kirkman, Kathryn Ryan, The Ranch, Crazy Ex-Girlfriend*, and more.

But at £7.99 a month, that's a bargain for JUST *House of Cards*!

And it's advert free!

Next gen consoles

You lucky, lucky S.O.Bs. Next gen consoles. Are you kidding me? And better is coming. If 16 year old me could see the quality, size, depth, emotion of what you have access to now, he would weep tears of joy. Now imagine what 40 year old you will think of the tech you have.

You have augmented reality and virtual reality about to kick in, in a massive way. The book *Read Player One* is becoming more realistic every year.
It's now not a "one size hero fits all" scenario. You can be a truly unique character, which has just as much opportunity and potential as anyone else.

You can create side quests that become the main quest, easily explore distant lands, and live any kind of life that you wish.

Your skills tree is no longer locked. You are coming out of formal education, and you can learn whatever skills you need, without having to wait for a DLC.

The world is yours! Explore it!

CHAPTER 9

Light In The Darkness

"Don't be ashamed to need help. Like a soldier storming a wall, you have a mission to accomplish. And if you've been wounded and you need a comrade to pull you up? So what?"

Marcus Aurelius

I purposely tried to keep this book short. Life is hard and time is our most precious commodity. Sure, we all might read a 500 page book for escapism or entertainment, but a book on what sounds suspiciously like homework? That's a tough sell and I get that.

My father, Trevor Horne, wrote a book called *Building Bridges: Embracing NLP for Better Mediation*. I am interested in NLP (Neuro Linguistic Programming) and I am more than happy to support my dad.

But I have not read it. Nope. Bad son standing right here.

But aaargh! It's a grown up book. It's a book for adulting, and corporations, and people who wear ties.

Its 282 pages (which I guess isn't that bad) with a grown up cover, and grown up chapter headings. So I haven't read it. My dad sent me a copy, and it's in my "to read" pile But I read other books instead. Shorter books. Easier to read books.

I am sure it's a great book, but it has the feel of work.

If you read it, let me know what you think.

Damn it. As I write this, I am convincing myself to start reading it.

Maybe I am not a bad son after all.

So. This book. It's a short fast read, full of signposts to help you find other sources that can help you on your quest. There is SO much choice out there, how do you know if something is worth reading, watching, playing, or listening too?

But you have read this far, so I guess you must at least like how I come across. Maybe we have a bit of trust going?

So here are my suggestions of books and TED talks that had a profound and deep impact on my life, and might be of interest to you too.

Book Recommendations

Reasons To Stay Alive by Matt Haig

This is an exploration of how Matt dealt with depression and anxiety. Be careful if you buy this. My wife cried when she saw I had it. So make sure those around you know what you are dealing with and maybe give them some reassurance.

But this is also worth reading even if you have no experience of anxiety or depression as it will give you a deep insight in to what the people who do have it, are going through.

This is a small book, quite a large font. Plenty of white space. Some chapters are a page long, others are a list of ten bullet points.

That's important. Because when you are depressed it's really hard to be motivated to do anything, but just maybe, maybe, you can read a one page chapter. And if you can do that…

It is honest, raw, hopeful, and funny.

Matt also makes it very clear that depression is one massive, mother of all monsters, dragon. It's a fight to end all fights. It's the major quest, the one you will need all your skills to win.

Do you know that point when you are deep into an RPG game and you keep getting killed by the same monster and so you make a decision. The decision to throw EVERYTHING you have at it.

Every spell, scroll, potion, consumable, weapon, and even companion.

That's the fight with depression.

Philosophy For Life and Other Dangerous Situations by Jules Evans

You probably are more aware of Stoicism than you think. You will have seen memes shared and liked on social media with a quote to help you get through the day.

Quotes by people such as Marcus Aurelius, Epictetus, and Socrates.

Those quotes are handy anchors to help deal with minor challenges of everyday life. But wouldn't you like to know a little more?

This is laid out like a day at university. With morning and afternoon lecturers by some of the key names in Stoic philosophy. It imagines that all these philosophers were teaching at the same school, and we get to learn about the different nuances and styles that are within the school of Stoicism.

Sure, not all of them appeal to me. Masturbating in public, for example. But there are real world examples of people using Stoicism in the modern world. Such as soldiers, nurses, etc.
You can use an ancient philosophy to deal with the modern world!

How amazing is that?

The Richest Man In Babylon by George S. Clason

While I was on a course in Edinburgh we were speaking about finances and debt, and one man talked about how he had gone bankrupt but was now doing very well. When asked what changed, he said that he had read this book.

I asked what it was called and made a mental note to one day get it, but not today – after all, a book on finances and history does not sound like fun.

But he then said that it was only a short book and held his thumb and forefinger apart about a centimetre. I ordered it that night.

Eleven chapters, that each tell a parable, set in Babylon.

It's easy to read, and actually quite simple. Budget, save, invest, passive income etc. Nothing you have not heard before, but because it is presented in a somewhat romantic way, it embeds deep.

Or at least it did with me. It felt like a new line of code had been added to my brain computer.

I understand those lessons, rather than just know them. Give it a go.

The Chimp Paradox by Professor Steve Peters

This book was mentioned in that same course in Edinburgh. It must have been in a room of very wise people indeed.

I recommend this probably more than any other book, because this will give you an understanding of how our minds work, and in what way we can hack them to be more successful, happy, and confident.

It's a simple premise. The author breaks down your brain in to three parts: the Monkey, Human, and Computer.

The Monkey is fearful, and wants security, and friends, and food and sleep and sex, amongst other things. It's also stronger than the human part, especially when it has not been trained. It is also even stronger at night, which is why we can blow things out of proportion in the early hours of the morning. The Monkey responds emotionally.

The Human responds logically, and has the job of listening to the Monkey, but also trying to act on what is for the best. Both of them look to the computer for core programming on how they should behave.

As a media specialist I am all too aware that we are (in part) a product of our programming, and so being given tips on how to write new code for my brain was like being given a super power.

Professor Steve Peters is insanely well-qualified, but this book is engaging, fun, and understandable. He talks about goblins and gremlins, which makes it all seem accessible.

The Writer's Journey by Chris Vogler

Of course this was going to be on the list! Chris emailed me back and gave me permission to quote this book. I love the book, and now I am a super fan of his. He didn't just reply, oh no. He replied and said he had read my Skyrim article and went on to talk about games he plays. He connected as a person (and a mentor).

So this is a guide for life. I spoke about it in chapter 2, but it really is worth reading the whole book. It's a big one, and I read it for university. However it is accessible and obviously goes into far more detail and gives more understanding than I ever could.

TED Talk Recommendations

One of my favourite things to do each new academic year is to introduce my students to TED talks. It is an insane resource of usually powerful short videos that focus on spreading ideas. They cover virtually every subject and can be funny, inspiring, fascinating, mind-blowing, and beautiful. Sure, not all of them will connect with you, but every so often one will completely change your perspective of the world.

There are well known, inspirational speakers that you would love to have as mentors. If they were doing a talk next door, you would go! People like Steve Jobs, Stephen Hawking, Richard Dawkins, Elon Musk, Bill Gates, Edward Snowden, Al Gore, and Julian Assange.

Here are a few of the talks I go back to year on year. It is no Surprise to me that they are some of the most watched in TED history.

Sir Ken Robinson

In my teaching community this guy's talks are spread around very regularly, and each time we see them we comment and share once more. He reminds us why we teach, and what we actually hope to achieve vs. endless admin and pigeon holing.

We know what a good education is. The leaders in our field know, the teachers know, and governments know. But for some reason, no government acts to implement it.

Check out Michael Moore's film *Where to Invade Next*; specifically when he looks at the education system in Finland.

The talk to start with is *Do Schools Kill Creativity?* I love the way he presents, because he does it through story telling.

Watch the talk. If the educational system let you down, it was not your fault. Put it behind you, and now move on to smash your life! You have time!

Amy Cuddy

I have mentioned Amy earlier in the book, and her TED talk has stirred up a bit of a debate questioning the science behind it. But my experience has been that there is some truth in what she says. How you hold your body, impacts your emotions. It can also impact the emotions of others.

This seems obvious to me, as it's so integral to media, filmmaking, acting... and even martial arts. We call it game face, and it goes back to Sun Tzu in the *Art of War*, "appear weak when you are strong and strong when you are weak."

Stand tall, shoulders back, in a Wonder Woman pose. Hold it for two minutes. Anything happen?

If not, may be you need different imagery.
But understanding body language is a cool life hack. Do you recognise how someone is trying to intimidate you? Or excuse you? It can be like playing chess, or rock/paper/scissors. You can counter it, if you recognise it.

Give her talk a watch and let me know what you think.

Andy Puddicombe

Andy is a mindfulness expert and founder of the app Headspace which helps with meditation. He juggles while he does a talk. How awesome is that? He does have a degree in circus arts though, which gives him an advantage. And he is a former Buddhist monk.

He talks about the last time you did nothing. Just sat. I find that fascinating as so many people need constant distraction. A phone, the TV, background music. Are you afraid to be alone, with your mind?

As well you might! Your mind has the capability to create your own personal hell, but you should not run from it you should manage it. But that takes some practice.

Andy gives a chilled discussion on how simple and achievable meditation and mindfulness can be.

It's about stepping back and observing your emotions in a relaxed and non-judgemental way. It's a great way to self-awareness and discovering a different perspective. You might not be able to change the world, but you can change how you experience it.

And he juggles. On stage. Giving a talk.

Shawn Achor

The Happy Secret to Better Work is a talk on happiness and potential. I love Shawn's fast-paced, humorous, delivery that tells personal stories. I love stories, and I think it's the best way to engage your audience. No one can be you better than you. You have no competition.

But what I particularly like about this talk, is I have found two earlier versions which were not quite as polished. It's the first time I fully understood that great public speakers practice. They hone the same talk, probably linked to their "why" and beliefs, until it is very slick.

Public speaking is like being a stand-up comedian, you should be practicing your material on friends, family, smaller audiences, up to larger stages.

The content of Shawn's talk is a wakeup call to how the fields of education, medicine, and psychology, want to pigeonhole us and make us average, or 'normal'.

He asks we change the way we seek happiness, as we are programmed to seek it from success. Success is always over the horizon because when we achieve something, we change the goalposts.

PERMISSION CREDITS

Bradberry, T (2017). 11 Habits of Mentally Strong People. Available: https://www.linkedin.com/pulse/11-habits-mentally-strong-people-dr-travis-bradberry. Last accessed 18th May 2017.

Harding, J. (2016). Children as young as 3 unhappy with their bodies. Available: https://www.pacey.org.uk/news-and-views/news/archive/2016-news/august-2016/children-as-young-as-3-unhappy-with-their-bodies/. Last accessed 18th May 2017.

King, R (2015). Full Contact Living. USA: Rodney King. 124.

Kruse, K (2016). Text Me!, Snap Me!, Ask Me Anything!. USA: The Kruse Group. Back Cover.

Kruse, K. (2017). About. Available: https://leadx.org/about/. Last accessed 18th May 2017.

Tait, P. (2015). 'How have we got education so disastrously wrong?'. Available: http://www.telegraph.co.uk/education/educationopinion/11568329/How-have-we-got-education-so-disastrously-wrong.html. Last accessed 18th May 2017.

Peter Tait © Peter Tait / Telegraph Media Group Limited;

Vogler, C (2007). The Writers Journey. 3rd ed. California: Michael Wiese Productions. 7.

Young Minds. Mental Health Statistics. Available: https://youngminds.org.uk/about-us/media-centre/mental-health-stats/. Last accessed 06th May 2017.

ONLINE RESOURCES

I know I have dropped a ton of references to speakers, films, interviews, and more. So I have made a YouTube channel with a collection of content you might find interesting.

You can find it as a play list on my YouTube account **@darrenhorne77**, or message me for a link.

I also have a Facebook group called ***The Level Up Squad,*** which is full of success minded people who want to get the most out of life. Come join us! If you can't find it on Facebook, message me for the link.

KEYNOTE SPEECHES

I have been teaching for over a decade and have developed a reputation for delivering engaging talks.

I have hosted and organised Q&As with filmmakers such as Ken Loach, Sybil Robson Orr, and John Hurt, as well as introduced a range of films at festivals.

I have also given talks on the Government's anti-terrorism strategy PREVENT with superb feedback.

"It was like a TED lecture on tolerance! Brilliantly done."

Paul Taylor, Co-Course Leader, Foundation in Art and Design

And I am often asked to do talks on motivation and equality and diversity issues.

In short, if you would like me to come and talk to your students, clients, or employees, just ask.

darrenhorne@live.co.uk

ABOUT THE AUTHOR

Darren Horne is a media and communication specialist working in post-compulsory education, in the UK.

He also owns and runs a martial arts studio focusing on life performance and self-preservation for mind and body.

He has recently started a life coaching business for 16-19 year olds and became a father to an amazing daughter in January 2016.

During the writing of this book he also became a contributor to www.LEADx.org, which seeks to help millennials get 1% better each day.

ACKNOWLEDGEMENTS

There are so many people to thank, and so little space. So I will focus of those that had a direct influence on this book.

A huge thank you to my media students, who continue to teach me, and keep me relevant. They have been incredibly supportive of this book, and have been encouraging me for years to move my career in the direction it is finally going.

Special thanks to Kasia Staniecka, Kieran Hunter, Alice Bell, and Lorna de Mello for motivating me, and giving valuable feedback every step of the way.

Big shout out to Josh Kotoff (Snapchat @mrscifiguy) who I have only known via Snapchat for a few months, and yet has been a superb ally. He introduced me to Hannah Raya (Snapchat @hammieraya) and he worked with her to create the book's storming cover design.

Then a firm handshake to my friend Tom Fallows, who took a break from his PHD on George Romero, and proofread this book, and gave me incredibly kind and generous critique and advice.

As did my father, Trevor Horne, and father in-law John Williams. Both read it on a very tight timescale and spotted typos and grammar mistakes, as well as giving insightful feedback.

If there are any grammar issues left, let's blame them. They are the grown-ups after all.

Shout outs also go to Phill Holden who has actively helped me believe in myself as a life coach, and to Darren Poole who did similar with helping me believe I could be an author.

In late 2016 I did a Neuro Linguistic Practitioner course which was ran by Lesley McDonald. That was an incredibly powerful experience, and led me to understand that I could re-program my mind to be happy. It was one of my key tools in the fight against depression and anxiety. How do you thank someone for that?

And also thanks to Kevin Kruse, Matt Haig, Gary Vaynerchuk, Erica Blair, Justin Kan, and Chris Vogler.

Sure I have never met any of you in person, but the content you put out, or the interactions we have had, continue to have a positive influence on me. Especially by setting the example of successful people happily reaching out, connecting, and helping others win, where they can. You guys rock!

As I type this we are packing up the apartment to move to a lovely house in a village, which Evie is going to LOVE. In an hour or two I will send this off to Amazon to get published, and in four days I hit forty years of age. Four decades!

It's a whole new stage of our lives, and I can't thank my wife Emily enough for riding out what was the worst time in our relationship. 2016 should have been amazing, but depression and anxiety nearly screwed it up entirely. I could easily be in an alternate universe in a small one bed flat, single, not writing this book, and feeling bitter and angry about the world. Or maybe TV's Katherine Ryan and I would have somehow got together.

And of course thank you to Evie. Bless you. Those who have been following our adventures on Snapchat will have seen how adorable she is, and how smitten I am with her. I fear I shall be at her beck and call for decades to come, and I wouldn't have it any other way.

And thanks to every one of you that bought the book, I hope you liked it. And if you did, an even bigger thanks if you left a review on Amazon or Good Reads. I suspect I will be reading every single one that is written.

Printed in Great Britain
by Amazon